D0925382

3 0600 00248 8469

CATAWBA:
OMENS, PRAYERS
& SONGS

CATAWBA: OMENS, PRAYERS & SONGS

poems by A. Poulin, Jr.

PUBLISHED IN PORT TOWNSEND BY
THE GRAYWOLF PRESS 1977

Published & printed by The Graywolf Press, Box 142, Port Townsend, Washington, with the aid of a grant from the National Endowment for the Arts.

ACKNOWLEDGMENTS

Grateful acknowledgment is due to the editors of *The American Poetry Review, Contemporary Literature in Translation* and *Mushroom* in which some of these poems first appeared.

The author and publisher are also grateful to Eric Sackheim, editor and publisher of Mushinsha Books, for permission to reprint these poems which are part of the book *The Widow's Taboo* to be published by Mushinsha Books.

And the author is particularly grateful to the National Endowment for the Arts and to the Research Foundation of the State University of New York for grants which made completion of these poems possible, as well as to the P.E.N. American Center for assistance in time of need.

Contents

Voice of a Language That Is Gone: A Prefatory Note

These are neither translations nor workings of original poems. Rather, I look upon them as "given poems" written while I was reading Frank G. Speck's *Catawba Texts* (Columbia University Press, 1934; A MS Press, Inc., 1969.)

Professor Speck's book is primarily an ethno-philological study—a collection of myths, tales, beliefs, charms, omens, prayers, taboos, medicine practices, social customs, industries, and occupations of the once great Catawba Nation of American Indians in North and South Carolina. Those 117 texts and variants were narrated by the only four remaining persons (three women and one man) who could express themselves in their native Catawba language during Speck's period of investigation between 1921 and 1931.

Some forty years after the original publication of *Catawba Texts,* Speck's scientifically sparse observation —"The language is gone"— assumes an even more stark and brutal dimension that conjurs an image of a nation without tongues, a communal spirit forever speechless, a people's exchange with creation forever silenced. It testifies to what extent the language of a people is as precious as it is fragile, utterly vulnerable to a kind of violence we still don't recognize or admit to.

As I read the literal translation of these texts,—a repetitious, awkward, and staccato syntax that is so alien to our historical sense of "style"—I was haunted by Professor Speck's own sense that they were "a last feeble voice from the grave of a defunct culture." But I was also moved by the feeling that behind that culture, under that syntax, there lives a voice confronting experience directly, openly, and with authentic mystery and humor: addressing a god, praying to an herb or an insect, recounting a moment of creation, or teaching virtue to a child with unguarded simplicity and honesty.

Stripped of culture's syntax and the exigencies of self-conscious artistry, this seemed to be a primal voice conversing with all creatures in the cosmos on equal terms, a voice we seldom hear or listen to, the root-breath and substance of poetry from a grave we all carry inside us.

A. Poulin, Jr.

for Daphne

if you repeat these tales
in the summer or the dark
a snake will be waiting
waiting to bite your tongue

Birds

birds are singing around my door
they're talking and singing
someone's coming someone's coming

Cardinal

look
the red bird just flew up

something's going to happen
something sudden unexpected
quick someone might even die

Money Birds

look
a flock of white money birds
tomorrow it will snow

Bluejay

the bluejay left on Saturday
he'll be gone three days
the bluejay will come back on Tuesday

he went to see the evil spirit
he took three grains of sand with him

Burning Sassafras

I'm burning sassafras
I'm burning grapevines
the moon is swallowing the smoke

I'll tell lies all summer
all the women will believe me

River Snake

my branch my son
don't go in the river

the snake in that water
is bigger than your mother

it'll wrap itself around you
and you'll never come back
you'll never never come back

Luck-Dreams

sometimes I dream of snakes
I know I won't be lucky
sometimes I dream of money
I know I will be lucky

what did you dream last night
was your dream good last night

last night I dreamt of nothing

Salamander

I heard a salamander
barking in the dark
I am going to die

Prayer to the Sun

tonight we go to bed
we've survived another day

tonight we go to bed
give us good light again
tomorrow thanks

Prayer after a Snakebite

foot of my first son
I'm rubbing you with milk
with the milk of a flower

let the poison out
let the poison flow
like blood like milk

the snake will go somewhere and die

Prayer to the Red Root

my nipples are cracked
my baby's hungry

I'm rubbing my nipples
with you red root

red root heal me
make my nipples soft
my baby eat

Prayer while Making Medicine

I've peeled the north side
of the medicine tree
let me make good medicine

oh you who never dies help
me I can't help myself

Hunter's Prayer

I'm going hunting
give me luck oh you who never dies

if I meet a woman on the way
I'll draw a cross on the ground
and spit on it I'll spit on it
for you who never dies

Prayer to the Turtle

I am eating your heart
I am eating your ancient heart
I will live a long long time
I will live a very long time
I will die very very hard

Hummingbird

the hummingbird was made by a man

he took a dandelion turned to seed
he held it in his hand and blew on it
yes and a hummingbird flew off

that man was very smart

Glass Snake

the glass snake stops
in the middle of the path
and thinks I'm hiding

hit it and it breaks
into pieces all in pieces
then each piece rolls back
glues itself into place
and the snake's alive again

but put the glass snake
in a fire a very hot fire
and it will shine
melting as it dies

Melon Patch

the land was good
I planted a melon patch
I drove sticks all around it
someone came to steal my melons
all my sticks turned into snakes

Hungry Birds

it was cold last night
and it snowed
the birds were hungry

today the sun is out
the rocks are warm
the birds are glad
they're singing in their nests

we'll make traps
catch the birds
and have something to eat

Whippoorwill

the whippoorwill
put a lady slipper
on his head and cried
spring is here

Possum Hunting

tonight we'll go hunting possum
we'll catch one and we'll eat it
bring a good dog and an axe
blow your horn cut down the tree

the possum climbed a big oak tree
it climbed a big and white oak tree
and I can't cut it down

Song of the Sick

I'm sick I'm very sick
put me to bed give me medicine
now all stand around me
stand around me and be happy
sing and dance around me
I'm already feeling better

Red Flower

we keep a red flower
in our house now
it will bring us luck
it will bring us gold
it will bring money in
our house a red flower

Dancing Ghosts

the sun has set it's dark
my father and mother
stand by the open door

across the river
where an ancient village
used to be someone's drumming
someone's drumming hard
people are singing and dancing

but no one's there
no one's been there for years
there is no one there

Widow's Taboo

your husband's dead
no one will talk to you
for one year your tongue
will be in his mouth

This volume was printed in an edition
of 740 copies, from hand-set Palatino type,
in winter, 1977. 100 copies are bound in boards,
signed and numbered by the poet; 640 copies are
smythe-sewn in paper wrappers.
The illustration is from Roy Nydorf's etching.